THE WAY OF
THE
CROSS

ISBN-13   Paperback   978-1-964100-77-7
            eBook   978-1-964100-76-0

Library of Congress Control Number: 2025905783

THE WAY OF THE CROSS

IKE WILLIAMS

W
O
HAVE NO FEAR   R   KEEP WALKING
S
H
I
P

And He said to them all,

"If any man will come after me,

let him <u>Deny</u> himself, and take up

his <u>CROSS DAILY</u> and follow me"

(Luke 9: 23 KJV)

FORWARD

There are no experiences on life's journey that are more exciting, perilous, and esoteric or rewarding, than when the Holy Spirit comes and takes control of someone's life. My life before that was no life at all. I was engaged in many things. My life had no specific direction, very little meaning and very little purpose.

This book chronicles some of the experiences that have transformed me since I surrendered my whole life to God through His Son Jesus Christ.

This work is also dedicated to my friend, and spiritual brother, Orson Smith, who has been faithful in his desire to serve God with all his heart. We walk together on this journey. Every step of the way there have been sacrifices, ups and downs, and setbacks, frustrations and even stagnation, but he never ceases to remind me that "Iron sharpens iron."

There were others who ventured on the journey with us, but diminished along the way.

In this experience we continue to grow in faith and in wisdom, knowledge and understanding through the abundant works of the Spirit of God in our lives through the love, mercy and grace of Jesus Christ.

John's Gospel ends with these words.

"And there are also many other
things which Jesus did
which if they were written every one,
I suppose that even the world itself could
Not contain the books that should be written
Amen"

John: 21 V-25 KJV

In the pages of this text are written some of the accounts of the work of the Holy Spirit in my life. I would not dare to say however, that my experiences with the precious Holy Spirit would fill volumes. What I can truthfully say though, is that my mind cannot comprehend nor contain the many experiences that I have had with the Holy Spirit even from birth, when I was born premature, and during the periods of my life when I had no interest or desire to know God; or wanted to have any relationship with His son Jesus Christ.

At the time of writing this book, twenty-six years have passed since my water baptism. Though years before that, in my youth, I somehow knew that God's presence was always with me. I cannot begin to explain the situations in my life that should have killed me, shattered me or destroy me. I now know, it was God's Grace that kept me. Back then, I was always running away from God, because I was clueless, not knowing that God was a loving father. (Which my fleshly father was not, he was not even active in my life). The problem was that in growing up, I was taught, or got the impression as did so many others in my generation and culture that God was a cruel task master; who was just sitting in heaven waiting for me to sin, so that He could punish me. To "hit me over the head with a big stick", in a manner of speaking. As a result, I grew up fearing God in a bad way, not knowing that one of God's divine nature is love beyond measure.

It was not until after I had lived over thirty years of my life that the change came. It was about this time that I left home to live in another country. Looking back now, it was most definitely the hand of God in operating. I viewed the move God orchestrated in my life similar to Abraham being called to leave his homeland to go to a place that God was directing him.

God, stripped me of my homeland, and my culture. I was a stranger in a foreign land, lonely and uncertain of the future.

Right then and there I knew I needed help, who else could turn to? Except Jesus. That was when I consciously gave my life to Christ. Why did I not do that before? Looking back now, I remembered that when I was in my late teens God had given me a revelation, which led me to believe in Him, yet I remained unmoved in my sinful self.

As much as I can remember, this was what happened. I was home sitting under a weeping willow tree in my garden reading the bible, why? I don't know, but been brought up in a Christian country, it was the norm for children to attend church and Sunday School, so Bible reading was a customary part of the culture. I don't recall what book of the Bible I was reading, but it must have been one of the Gospels, because what I was reading spoke about God sending His only begotten Son to die for sinners.

I paused and thought, who would do that? What kind of God is this? I knew from going to church and Sunday school that Jesus died on the cross for us, but it never dawned on me like it did that morning reading about it under the weeping willow tree. It took my breath away. As I pondered that great sacrifice in my heart, tears welled up in my eyes, and for the first time in my life a flicker of understanding God's love for me melted my heart. I thought to myself if God loved me so much, the least I could do was love Him back.

That was the extent of my conversion because I never repented, never went back to church, which I had stop attending since the age of fifteen, or became a Christian.

I just continued living the way I did, but somehow I knew that something was planted in my heart.

To deliver me, from myself, God intervened in my life, and as mentioned before, like Abraham moved me to a new life. Here I found myself isolated, it was like being on the backside of the mountain like Moses, cut off from my culture and familiar faces. Cut off from distractions and interferences which I had constructed to hide from God. Here in the new land, I found myself with lots of free time, and this was when God began through the Holy Spirit to work deeper depths and higher heights in my knowledge and understanding of Him. Wow! God works in mysterious ways, His wonders to perform. I do believe I would have died and not known God if I had left to worship the god I had created in my old life.

 In my new country, I began growing in my relationship with God, as I worked tirelessly with the youth ministry in the church where I became a member. Years went by, then one Sunday after service a brother in the church gave me a ride home, and then questioned, if I would be interested in joining him and a few other brothers in early Morning Prayer and Bible readings.

I jumped at the opportunity, as at the time I was hungering for something more than just going to church on Sundays, prayer meetings on Wednesdays and helping out in youth ministry on Fridays. I expressed the fact that if we were going to do this we should be seriously committed. My brother who came up with the idea on the other hand, had reservation about his faithfulness, nonetheless we decided to step out, and might I add not in faith. Looking back though, I know that God gave the measure of faith necessary for us to make that initial first step, though there was trepidation on our part, I however felt more confident than my friend. He however knew that he initiated the move, so turning back was out of the question. Why? Because he prides himself to be a man of his words. However, we had no clue that the way of the cross was going to be so heavy. The best thing though, was that we were not carrying our crosses alone, every step of the way God's Holy Spirit was there to comfort and guide as we began to learn how to cast every care upon Him. It has been a journey that still continues to this day, in which we are continually taught incredible spiritual knowl-edge, as we keep walking, and growing in the Holy Spirit.

The plan was that we would meet the first week in every month at five am: at the church. During this week we would fast, and the fast would not be broken until at the end of the week on Friday, after three in the afternoon. This we did constantly for six or seven years.

However, for whatever reason, as we continued some of the brothers fell by the wayside, leaving only three of us in the group. It was unbelievable the revelations and spiritual growing that began taking place during these sessions of the first week of every month, fasting, praying and reading the Bible. One of the outstanding memorable things among many other memorable things that I recalled was the name the Holy Spirit gave us.

 One morning during one of our meetings a revelation came to me that we were the 'OIL.' I was puzzled, "what are you saying?" my mind asked. When the Holy speaks it is often something that one would never have thought of in a million years. Oil? I pondered again, "yes," He replied. The letters in your first names when put together spell oil. Orson, Ike and Leroy. "Well blow me down!" I thought again. Oil? "Yes." When I told this revelation to my other two brothers, they were as astounded in much the same way as I was.

As my mind journeyed back to that moment, I now begin to really reflect on the significance of oil. Anointing oil is mentioned in the Bible twenty time. Oil consecrates, oil purifies, oil is one of the fuel that facilitates light and oil heals. In Mark 6:13 the oil is used for the blessing and healing of the sick.

In James 5: 14 the people were encouraged to call for the elders of the church to anoint and bless any who was sick. Oil is associated with so many sacred activities. In Psalm 23, David states that God anoints his head with oil, which blessed him so much that his cup 'runneth over.' Anointing oil goes back to the time of the Children of Israel in the wilderness, when Moses was instructed by God to anoint Aaron as high priest. No one could be separated to the priesthood unless anointed with oil. The tradition of anointing priests and kings became a fundamental part of the Jewish tradition in order to make them eligible for their office. Saul and David were anointed kings.

I do not exactly know what God was doing when that revelation was given to me, but I firmly believed, that God was doing something special within us and in our lives. Rain or shine, cold or hot, or even when we felt like throwing in the towel we kept going. To me this was like a covenant relationship. I remembered a time when I had car problems and 'L' had to come and get me in the mornings. He had a leaking radiator, so by the time he got to me he had to pop the hood of his car to pour water in the radiator, and after our meeting, he again had to repeat the action to get me home and repeat the action again to get himself home.

This continued for a while till his car went down, then 'O' had to take up the baton. The frustrating thing was that 'O' lived a few miles East of the church and we lived a few miles West of the church. That means in order for us to meet at our usual hour, and get back home in time to get ready for work, 'O' had to get up extra early. There were other obstacles, but God always made a way.

As a teacher it was a challenge for me to stick to my first week of the month fast. This was because I was always around children who were always eating. Some came to school with breakfast they purchased on their way, from one of the fast food places. At snack time they ate, at lunch time they ate, and even after school while they waited for parents to pick them up they would be eating left over snacks from their lunches, or snacks they purchased from the tuck shop. I could not get away from the temptation of eating during the first week of every month.

There were times when children in my class would celebrate their birthdays with a class party, which I would have to supervise, sometimes I would have to cut the cake or pass out drinks and other foods, even when parents were present. I think it was only a part of the training of overcoming temptation. I must admit though, I was not always successful, sometimes, it was when the food was already in my mouth that I remembered that I was on a fast. Too late!

I can imagine God smiling at the struggles we had to go through in order to become stronger, and the saints of heaven looking over the balcony of heaven encouraging us to fight on. The Spirit never stopped giving revelations. Another revelation came to me one morning while we were about to wrap up our meeting. There were three things that the Spirit told me to do, which was instructions for all of us. This was what was impressed on my heart.

'Keep Walking'

'Have no Fear'

'Keep Praising'

I cannot remember if they came in that order. But those Instructions became our watch words and the foundations on which we stand on to this very day, and the pillars that support our faith.

When I communicated this revelation to my brothers they were again, just as astounded like me. As we began to ponder the meanings of the instruction, 'O' said,

"A threefold cord is not easily broken" As we carried on our six to seven years of fasting, reading, and praying for the first week in every month 'board meeting' (as we called it) with the Holy Spirit, I noticed that every time a revelation was given to me, it was a threefold instruction.

Let me pause here to say that after a while, "I can't remember exactly when," only 'O' and 'I' were continuing on this journey.

We were a little concerned about this break up when 'L' stopped coming. We could no longer consider ourselves 'OIL.' This was kind of disappointing to us. 'O,' however came up with a solution which was sort of funny. He said "since there is no longer any 'L' in the 'OIL,' the Holy Spirit would now be the 'L.' I was relieved to hear that, because we both could still consider ourselves as 'OIL,' because our Lord and savior Jesus Christ through His spirit completed the group. "Wherever two or three are gathered in my name;

I am in the midst to bless." Indeed the 'L' in the 'Oil' was truly the presence of the spirit of the Lord Jesus Christ.

'Keep walking, have no fear, and keep praising' are such deep spiritual truths that I would like to spend some time here pondering each instruction.

KEEP WALKING;

Keep walking is more figurative than literal. Though sometimes one has to physically move to get what God wants to be done. Most often though, the walk is spiritual, mental or emotional, but this is what builds strength, faith and self-control or discipline. One of the most important issues that Christians struggle with is to know the will of God for their lives. That revelation usually doesn't come overnight. It is a process. If any Christian wants to know the will of God for his life or her life; that individual will have to keep walking with God.

The concept of keep walking is so deep, I don't think I have the capacity to reveal the depth of what God intends when He gave that instruction. If I were a theologian I think I would be better able to give a lengthy exegesis on the topic, but here is my interpretation of what I understood God to be telling us, when he instructed us to *'keep Walking.'*

Many Christians stay in the same place in their relationship with God. "Saved and stuck." God, is a God that keeps expanding in our hearts, and in our experiences. The more we know of God, is the less we know about Him. The song writer says "God is so high you can't get over Him, He is so wide you can't get around Him, so low you can't get under Him." It is Ludacris that so many Christian are satisfied with just going to church once or twice per week, some even less, and honestly believe that they know God.

This walk cannot be motivated by what we see in the physical. The Bible teaches that we must walk by faith and not by sight. This walk therefore is a walk of faith. This walk is also a walk-in love, because God is love. To me the most important activity in this walk, is to learn to walk like Jesus. When you keep walking with God, life becomes an exciting adventure; though, sometimes fearful, and painful. We just never know what to expect. But one thing I eventually came to really understand is that God is faithful, and that He will never leave us nor forsake us; although His ways are far above ours. The scripture teaches, 'As far as the East is from the West, so high above our ways are God's ways.' God has so many doors to open and close in our lives. Many times, we wrestle with God when he begins to close doors, because we have become so comfortable with that space or place we find ourselves in, that we don't want to vacate it.

God closes doors for us to keep walking, for us to keep moving. When that thing or circumstance has served its purpose, it is time to pull up stakes. The Children of Israel always knew when it was time to pull up stakes. When it was time to pack up and continue the journey, God would direct them by a pillar of cloud by day or a pillar of fire by night. God's Spirit led them.

Often my walking is done in stillness. In communion with the Holy Spirit. It is in these times of quiet mediation, prayer, reading the word or in fellowship with 'O' that God reveal to us the path, the plan, the purpose, the direction. There will never be a time when we will reach a place where we will say, "This is it." We are done walking. It is graduation time. No! For with God there will always be deeper depths, and higher heights to reach. Because God is always stretching us, perfecting us. The journey will never be finished till we stand face to face before God to give an account, to hear "Well done my good and faithful servant..." or, "Depart from me, I know you not."

The walking never stops. The thought, that at some point in my journey, I may come to the place of believing that 'This is it', is one of the obstacles that hinders my walking; tempting me to believe that I have reached the place where I should pitch my tent. Many people refer to this place as retirement. A place where we come to after working hard for most of our lives. This is where we can sit back, 'kick off our shoes,' and say to ourselves, "we have arrived." The reality is that there is no such place in Christ. When we retire from our jobs, the work of God continues. The destination, the end game is eternity.

As we keep walking we are going to encounter new situations, new experiences and new challenges, either physically, mentally or emotionally. We know we are walking when we find ourselves in situations where our trust in God begins to be shaken; when we begin to doubt, when our faith begins to feign.

When we feel ourselves been drawn out of our comfort zone, make no mistake that this is the time when our worst enemy begins to attack.' Fear!' It will begin to creep in. Sometimes in my walk, all I have the faith to do, is to put one foot in front of the other to keep moving. It is just like going jogging, sometimes I feel like I am going to die if I don't stop, and all I think of at that time, is just keep putting one foot in front of the other to get me through completing the course.

Doubt and fear are two sides of the same coin. Both walk hand in hand, step by step, so when you begin to doubt God, know that fear is right behind that feeling of doubt. Psalm 23 states "…. Yea though I walk through the valley of the shadow of death I will fear no evil, for thou art with me …" The more we walk with God, the closer we are drawn to Him. The more we walk with God the more self-dies.

I have also come to the realization that even if in my walking I find myself in a temporary stationary position, my walking must be continued in the word of God. That is, I must continue reading my Bible, and keep walking in my spirit, finding new revelations, and inspirations even in passages of familiar Scriptures. My desire is to walk with God like

Enoch. I want to walk with God till I am no more, which is no more on the earth, but caught up with God in the spirit.

Walking with God, is to be in conscious and consistent conversation with the Holy Spirit; as I go through my daily activities, I find that it is an exercise of walking in love. I have to constantly remind myself to be patient and not become irritable. In short, it is carrying my cross daily. Walking with God also means not boxing God in. We often put God in a box when we believe that the way God worked for us in the past is the same way He is going to work for us presently or in the future.

 As I walk, I must also be conscious of the traps and pitfalls that the enemy has set for me, but the Holy Spirit opens my eyes to see, and I am very thankful that in these times God has provided a way of escape.

HAVE NO FEAR;

Fear is a natural emotion not only for humans but also for animals. So many people learn and experience this emotion even before they know and experience love. Fear is a crippling emotion, it imprisons, it debilitates, and it destroys. The biggest weapon of the enemy is fear. The world today has become engulfed in fear. It prevents God's best for his people. It is no surprise that the Bible encourages us not to fear. 'Fear not' is the most repeated command in the Bible. In fact, it has been said that there are 365 "fear not's" in the Bible – one "fear not" for every day of the year.'

Lloyd Agilvie, <u>In Facing the Future without Fear,</u> even said that, "there are 366 'fear not's" in the Bible, one for each day of the year, including leap year" <u>Google.com.</u>

Revelation 21: 8 states that 'the fearful shall not inherit the Kingdom of God.' From this passage of scripture, it shows how dangerous it is for believers to operate in fear. Fear cancels faith, and again the Bible teaches that 'without faith it is impossible to please God' (Hebrews 11:6) because anyone who comes to Him must believe that He exists, and that he rewards those who earnestly seek Him. Faith cancels fear and fear cancels faith. Both work on each other.

I am sure that thousands of people can testify that they have missed many golden opportunities in their lives because of fear. We fear that we don't have enough money, we fear sickness, we fear death, we fear for our children, we fear for our families, some fear flying, and some of us even fear each other, and the list goes on. Love is the antidote for fear. God is love. If that fact is truly understood and embraced no one would fear. 'Perfect love cast out fear.' (John 4:18).

There is no one who gives perfect love except God, He is the Agape lover. Oh, if we really could understand that. 'if God is for us, who can stand against us?' then we would not fail at the things we do, if they are done in His will. When I truly believe that 'The Lord is my light and my salvation, then whom shall I fear? When I truly believe that the Lord is the strength of my life, then of whom (or what) shall I be afraid?' (Psalm 27), it is then, that I find the peace that passeth understanding. When confronted by fear, to overcome it, I remind myself that God has not given me a spirit of fear, but a spirit of love and a sound mind. (2 Timothy 1:7)

I do not walk in fear anymore because I know I am sheltered. Sheltered because I am covered in the blood of Jesus. Sheltered because I dwell in the house of the Lord, and He hides me in His pavilion, in the secret of His tabernacle. Sheltered because I walk in the shadow of the almighty. Sheltered because He covers me with His feathers, sheltered because He hides me in the cleft of the rock, and that rock is Jesus. So, though the terror by night may come, or the arrow that flyeth by day, or the pestilence that lurks in the darkness, or the destruction that comes at mid-day, or a thousand falling by my side and ten thousand at my right hand, I will not fear because the Lord is my habitation. That is where I live. I am sheltered, 'safe on His gentle breast.'

Having no fear helps me to experience the abundant life God has for me, because I lean not to my own understanding; in all my ways I acknowledge Him and He directs my path. When I learn to eliminate fear from my life, it is like entering a whole new world with endless possibilities. The scripture that says, 'I can do all things, through Christ who strengthens me, encourages me. That thought has taken on a new meaning, becoming flesh, and dwelling in me. What could I do, if I did not fear failing?

Eliminating fear from my life is like casting off a heavy burden I have been carrying all my life. There are so many great things I would have accomplished in my life, had it not been for the fear factor, but thanks be to God; I am now truly immune from that awful weapon of the enemy. 'FEAR.' It does not control me like it used to.

When you take your eyes off the word of God, fear takes control. Fear overcame Peter on his way walking on water to Jesus. When he became overwhelmed by fear, and took his eyes off Jesus he began to sink. As I keep my eyes on Jesus through the word of God it dismantles any fear that tries to swallow me up. When Peter took his eyes off Jesus, and began to look at the wind and waves in the storm, he feared and began to sink. Keeping our minds and thoughts on Jesus helps us to overcome fear.

Luke 12:6-7 'Are not five sparrows sold for two copper coins? And not one of them is forgotten before God. But the very hairs of your head are all numbered. Do not fear therefore; you are of more value than many sparrows.' Here the scripture is saying, that if God can care so much for the sparrows that are worth almost nothing, how much more does he care for us. That thought alone, should make us fearless.

The only fear that Christians should have is the fear of God. 'And I say to you, my friends, do not be afraid of those who kill the body, and after that have no more that they can do. But I will show you whom you should fear; Fear him who, after He has killed, has power to cast into hell; yes, I say to you fear Him!' (Luke 12: 4-5). Fear God, here don't mean to be afraid of God, but it means to be in awe of God, be in excessive wonders of His supernatural powers. Today the only fear I walk in is the fear of knowing the infinite powers of God, yet so loving, awesome, merciful, and gracious. The fear of God, is the beginning of all wisdom' (Proverbs 9: 10).

Fear of God is coming into the understanding of the depth of the holiness of God. God is so holy, that no matter how devout and faithful a Christian I become I can never, never come close to the holiness of God. My fear of God makes me love Him more.

KEEP PRAISING;

"God inhabits the praises of His people"

God is a jealous God; (Exodus 20), He wants us worshipping no other Gods but Him.

"His jealousy is aroused by His love for us," states Addison D. Bevere in his book

<u>Saints; Becoming More Than "Christian."</u> Bevere continues to say, "If we refuse to worship Him the rocks will transform into something greater and find breath to sing His song." He also states that, "The brilliance of our humanity grows in our worship of God." "When we lose sight of this truth, we worship the creation rather than the Creator – which is the essence of idolatry and the birthplace of sin, separating us from the life, love, and promise found in the knowledge of God's true form and purpose."

"There is no greater worship than dying to self. It is the only thing that will free us from sin…." Addison D. Bevere.

Psalm 100, states we should "Enter His gates (of worship) with thanksgiving, and into His courts with praise…."

Psalm 150 tells how we are to worship and praise God. It ends by saying V: 6 "let everything that hath breath praise the lord. "Praise ye the Lord."

It is said that "when the praises go up the blessings will come down." When we worship and praise God we create an atmosphere for God's glory to descend. He reaches down and makes Himself available to us. Worship washes our spirits and refreshes our souls, it helps to strengthen us to carry on. Worship makes the place on which we stand Holy. And we should understand that we are in the awesome presence of the Lord God Almighty, Creator of the universe.

The words of one of my favorite worship song are;

> *"Come let us worship and bow down,*
> *Let us kneel before the lord our God our maker*
> *For He is our God, and we are the*
> *people of His pastures and*
> *The sheep of his hand. "*

Worship is a form of love. It is the time we set apart to tell God how much we love and adore Him. We can't love God enough, in the same way that we can't Worship and praise Him enough. Worship transports us in the holy and glorious presence of God. As in the words of Psalm 63: 3; we are reminded '*Because thy loving kindness is better than life, my lips shall praise thee.*" Worship satisfies our souls.

"*My soul shall be satisfied as with marrow and fatness; and my mouth shall praise thee with joyful lips.*" Psalm 63: 5. When we constantly praise and worship God it helps to take our minds off the things of the world. Then we will be surprised 'that the things of the world will become strangely dim in the light of His glory and grace.' (The words from the song 'turn your eyes upon Jesus')

As Christians we should find immense pleasure in every opportunity we have to praise and worship God, not just when we go to church, or when we wake up in the mornings, or when we go to bed at nights. Throughout the course of our day, we should pause to worship God, thanking Him for His Grace and mercy. When we get to heaven that is all we are going spend every waking moment doing. It would be unlikely that we will ever sleep. Like the twenty four elders and the beasts around the throne of God in Revelation chapter 4: 10 -11, KJV, we will "*fall down before Him that* 'sits' *on the throne, and worship him that liveth forever and ever, and cast* 'our' *crowns before him saying,*

"Thou art worthy,
O lord,
To receive glory and honor and power:
For thou hast created all things,
And for thy pleasure they are and were created."

Worship cause our trials and tribulations to dissipate. When we go to worship God we are to be very sure that our praise and prayer basket outweighs and counterbalances our basket of despair and worry. Our worship basket must be full to overflowing. We must praise and pray without ceasing.

Sometime in 2011 I became very ill, and was hospitalized. This was about the sixth or seventh year after we had started our first week in every month early Morning Prayer, Bible reading, and fasting. This was one of the reasons, but not the only reason why we stopped meeting and engaging in what we have been doing so consistently over the past six to seven years. The other reasons were that our church was going through some fundamental changes. The founding pastor was offered the position of senior pastor in a more established congregation within the same denomination. Many of the members left and followed him. A new pastor from outside our congregation took over, much to the dismay of those of us who were expecting someone from our flock to take over the leadership. Those were some of the issues that led to the termination of meeting at the church.

When that season of meeting at the church ended, another season started which my brother 'O' and 'I' are still continuing to this day. We decided to meet every Saturday Mornings at six a.m.

When we first started this new season, our meeting place was on the beach. We lived on an island so the beaches were never more than a mile or two away, depending on which beach we decided on each Saturday morning. However we mostly went to one particular beach until it was closed to public access.

When that happened we found another suitable beach. After sometime, that too was closed off from public access to facilitate some kind of construction for tourist attraction. We then relocated to another area not on the beach this time but close to one. In a semi-wooded area which looked out on the Atlantic Ocean.

These were turbulent times for us. At one point we both were unemployed. We found ourselves in a dark place. What I have learned about the dark place, from listening to an interview with Pastor Michael Todd on TBN (Trinity Broadcasting Network) is that the dark place is where God develops us. It is like the dark room of a photographer's studio, where in the old days photographs were developed in dark rooms from films. Not at all like today where people just take out their phones and snap pictures. Joyce Myers, also said that God gives treasures in the dark.

In this time God was stripping us, molding us, cutting and reshaping us even more. It was hard, it was scary, it was lonely, but through it all God remained faithful, He never left us nor did He forsook us. My brother felt it more acute than I, because he has a big family, and he at that time was the only bread winner.

Despite the various adversities we still kept our Saturday Morning 'board meeting' appointments with the Holy Trinity. We continued meeting until my brother 'O' got employment on another island, the capital island of our country. Meanwhile, I was re-employed after I had taken early retirement. We were not troubled by this separation, because this was answered prayers, as we both were unemployed for I can't remember how long. We knew without the shadow of a doubt that it was God who had opened these doors.

Thank God for technology, because we were still able to meet by phone every Saturday mornings at six a: m, talk to each other, encourage each other, pray and do Bible study. We are no longer just reading random scriptures. We have become more mature in God, so we are now studying specific books and specific themes. The Psalms are incredible, they really reveal to me, how God is mighty, and how He is to be worshipped.

I don't have enough words or time to tell of the spiritual and miraculous experiences we have had as we continued meeting with the Holy Spirit of God during our Saturday Morning 'board meetings' on the beaches, to now by phone.

From when we started at the church till now, it has been way over twenty years. We have stopped counting. In the same way in which we have stopped counting how many times we have read the Bible from Genesis to Revelation. I am not saying this for accolades. I am simply saying this because of how alive and active the word of God is. No matter how many times we read through the Bible, there is always something mind blowing and exciting to discover. At the moment that I am writing this text we are studying the Book of Daniel, and the theme 'End Time prophecy.'

Let me just take a breath here and tell you of another three prong revelation the Spirit of God directed me to practice during these times. His direction to me is never in an audible voice. It is like something illuminating me from the inside.

One of the things I do regularly early on a Sunday Morning is to go jogging to the beach, which is not far from my home, maybe a mile or a little less. I jog to the beach, exercise for about two hours and then go swimming in the ocean. I only go in the water when the weather is warm. I do not go in the water during the cold months from January to May.

On one of those Sunday Mornings when I was engaged in my exercise, these words were dropped into my spirit. *'Eat right, exercise, pray.'* Right away I knew where the thought came from. It was from the Holy Spirit. I knew the peculiar feeling when something is whispered in my mind that is not from my own intellect. I paused my routine, and started to ponder what was said to me. When these inspirations come to me, I know I am being given principles to live by. This was a profound instruction, as to what I must do in order for me to have longevity to carry out the will of God throughout my life.

My human mind began to dissect the instruction. *'Eat right, exercise, pray.'* I began to examine the logics of the commands. I don't believe any sane person on this planet is unaware of the tremendous value and benefits of eating right and exercising. In addition, everyone I believe, especially Christians and other religious people know of the power of prayer. The thing is, there is a difference between knowing and doing. However, not just doing, but making a thing a regular part of one's lifestyle is the challenge. After finishing my meditation on the revelation I came away believing that this was another lifestyle principle God was adding to our spiritual journey; the journey that 'O' and myself are on.

One cannot doubt the value of this instruction, not just for me, but for every living breathing soul. God's words are for the individual as much as it is for everyone who hungers and thirsts after Him. In His word God has given us clear instructions of what to eat, Genesis: 1: 29 KJV is one of the first places where God tells us what to eat. *"And God said, I have given you every herb bearing seed, which is upon the face of all the earth, and every tree, in which is the fruit of a tree yielding seeds; to you it shall be for meat."*

In Leviticus Chapter 11 God again gave to Moses and Aaron strict instructions of what the children of Israel should and should not eat. It is very clear that God wants us to eat the natural things from the earth. In today's society most of the foods people consume are grown by using chemicals that are harmful to the human body, and kept edible by harmful preservative. Many of the illnesses and diseases that plague mankind is the result of not eating right. Our modern culture thrives on fast food, which has way too much fat, and sodium, and lacks essential vitamins and minerals. In some cultures people are accustomed to eat unclean animals which cause serious diseases that even lead to pandemic.

I have been trying my best to eat right. But not only to eat right, but also to pray over my food, giving thanks for it, and also praying for those who don't have. I try to record each week the amount of live foods I eat in comparison to dead foods. Live foods are food in which the natural prosperities, like vitamins, minerals and enzymes are not destroyed by cooking. Dead foods are cooked food. I therefore try to make fruits, vegetables, fruit juices and nuts priority in my diet.

If the body is not fed correctly then bodily exercise becomes almost impossible, burdensome, and intimidating. Food provides energy for the body to function, because the body was made to move. That is why we have muscles and joints.

The great commission from Jesus is to go out into the world to teach, preach, and make disciples. How can we do that if our bodies are not fit? There is so much more that could be added to the subject of eating right and exercising if we want to stay in the game of been used purposeful by God. He has a plan for us, but because He has given us free choice we often mess up the plan by simply not eating right and exercising, surrendering to the lust of the flesh.

Pray the third part of the instruction. Prayer is like oxygen to our spirits. Just as in the way that oxygen depravity caused physical death, so too does prayer depravity causes spiritual death. That is why the Bible admonishes us to "rejoice always, pray without ceasing, and give thanks to in all circumstances. 1st Thessalonians 5:16 -18.

I really try to pray without ceasing, why, because I sin unconsciously. In thought words and deeds, in things I have done, and things I have left undone. Knowing that Christ can make his second appearance at any time, and also that I can die at any time, I don't want to be found wanting. I am trying to live rapture ready, as a bride without spots or wrinkles, and unceasing praying is one sure way of keeping me rapture ready, because without prayer I certainly cannot do anything in my own strength.

Another scripture that also encourages me to pray ceaselessly is found in Luke 18:7. "And He spoke a parable unto them to this end that men ought always to pray and not faint." In this parable Jesus tells the story of the widow and the judge, in which the widow keeps going back to the judge daily, until he gets tired of her, fearing she would wear him down so, he eventually grants her request. From this parable Jesus is instructing us to never give up on praying, because

God will surely answer in His time. God hears and answers prayers. Sometimes the answer is not what we want to hear. It is sometimes yes, no, or wait. The prayers of the saints are lifted up to God as a sweet smelling incense.

There is a saying that states that prayer changes things. That is because God hears and works through prayer. He also delights in our prayers, because it is a sacrifice to Him.

Permit me to share one more revelation before I close this text. The instructions given to me this time concern the reading of the Bible. I was instructed that when I read the Bible, I should not consider or view it as an ancient document, stationed in antiquity, but instead read it, and examine it in context of what is happening in today's world.

The other instruction is that as I read, open my spiritual ears to listen and hear what God is saying to me personally. God is always speaking. I often hear many Christians say, God has never spoken to them. That is not true if we read the word and mediate upon it, we will hear His still small voice. God also speaks to us through nature that is around us, if we take the time to look and listen.

"Those who have eyes to see let them see; those who have ears to hear let them hear."

The journey my friend and I have embarked on, to follow in the footsteps of Jesus over twenty years ago was not orchestrated by us. It was ordained by the power of the Holy Spirit.

There is so much we have learned on this journey as we keep walking. Some of what we have learned I will try to explain here.

I did not give my life to Christ until I was forty years old. Something I regret, when I know now what I have missed out on in all those years trying to live buy my rules and the dictates of the world. Thinking I was living, when in fact I was dead. I now know why it took me so long. As I stated earlier on, growing up we were taught in my culture that God was basically sitting in heaven waiting for us to sin so He could punish us. We were not taught that God was a loving God. My world view was that God was an angry God. A vengeful God, whose delight was to condemn us to hell. So, I was afraid of God, and my intention was to run away and hide from Him.

When I came to the knowledge that God's nature is love, every time I err, I hurry to His outstretched arms asking forgiveness. Consider this; we were born in sin and shaped in inequity. So how can a God who has died to take us out of such a condition, be about putting us back there? That makes no sense! I have come to understand that God does not put sin on us. God don't have anything to do with sin, except to forgive us of it, and take us out of it. It is we who condemn ourselves to sin by breaking God's laws. Disobedience has consequences. If you run the red light and get hit by a car, are you going to blame the red light? Are you going to blame the other driver? Of course not. You broke the law, you pay the price.

Another important lesson I have learned in my relationship and walk with God, is how big God is, and how we have limited Him in our finite humanity. For God to get us to know and understand Him, He came in human flesh in the form of His Son Jesus Christ. As a result, we have the tendency to want to relate to God based on how we relate to each other as humans. We have no clue of the holiness and the depth of God's love toward us. It boggles the mind. To think that God created the universe and knows the individual names of the billions and billions of stars in limitless space, and knows the number of hair on our heads; who is man that He is mindful of us? We don't know how to make the limitless God expand in our humanity and do the great and marvelous things that He wants to accomplish in our lives. We have to learn how to expand ourselves in the greatness of our God who is the Alpha and Omega.

I have now learned also what it means, and how to cast all my cares upon Jesus. Before this, I often prayed that the beauty of Jesus be seen in me. This never seems to work, because often when I would catch a glimpse of my face in a mirror it would appear depressed, burdened and sad. Ironically that was not how I was feeling on the inside. But the feeling was just not penetrating the outside. Why was my face not reflecting the beauty of Jesus? I figured that I was not really casting my cares on Jesus, I was only saying it. If I were really casting my care on Jesus I should be all smiles, why? Because "the joy of the Lord is my strength."(Nehemiah 8:10). Now when I say I am casting my cares on Jesus I wear a smile on my face, and whenever the smile begins to fade, because of the challenges and concerns of daily living; I get a weird feeling. It is if my brain starts to wrinkle like the skin of a prune, causing my face to look unhappy and haggard. As I become aware that this is happening I put the smile back on, and I immediately I feel like my brain smoothing out, like the skin of a healthy grape.

I now know that casting my cares on Jesus means casting everything. If I start worrying about something, I cast it on Jesus. If someone hurts my feelings, I cast it on Jesus. If I fail at doing something I cast it on Jesus and then plaster a smile back on my face to convince myself that my cares are on Jesus.

When I constantly practice casting my cares on Jesus I know I am practicing living in the presence of God. "In God's presence there is fullness of joy, and at His right hand are pleasures forevermore" (Psalm 16:11).

One of the things that gives me most joy in my relationship with the Holy Spirit of God; is to help people understand eternity. Life is but a vapor. Eternity has no end. I want people who do not know Christ, to know that eternity has only two destinations. Eternal life or eternal death. How we live our lives in the here and now is preparing us for where we are going to spend eternity. If I am not remembered for nothing else in my life. I would like to be remembered as an individual whom through the power of the Holy Spirit has helped people understand the great blessings of eternal life.

I know that there is still so much more to learn from things yet unrevealed. Thank God, He has removed the fear. We have grown to love God more intimately, knowing without a doubt that 'we can take Him at His word.' We started out with mustard seed faith, but now it has grown beyond that. Thank you Jesus.

God's words cannot return to Him void, and we know that heaven and earth will pass away if just one punctuation mark in God's word is taken out of place.

There is a song that states;

"The longer I serve Him the sweeter he grows,

The more that I love Him more loves He bestows…"

That definitely has been our experience on this walk. Sometimes when I look back on the journey, I only see. "One set of footprints in the sand," then I rejoice and sing "Learning to lean, on Jesus being, safe and secure from all alarm…."

At the risk of sounding cliché the prerequisite for this journey is "letting go and let God." Self has to die. Not just die, self has to be crucified with Christ.

So my brother and I can now say without hesitation, it is not we who live, but it is Christ through His Holy Spirit that lives in us.

By saying that, I remember one of my brother's fervent prayer is always asking God to let the mind of Christ be in us. This is how he states it. "Lord let your Holy Spirit sandwich us from the world."

Many people even Christian are afraid to take up the cross and follow Jesus. There is a saying, "No cross no crown." A song writer asks this question.

"Must Jesus bear the cross alone and all the world go free?

His answer is no, "For there is a cross for you and for me." There is an old song that goes like this;

"If you only knew the bless-
ings that Salvation brings,
You would never, never stay away,
If you only saw the table spread
with lovely things
You would come to the feast today.
For the door is opened wide and
the Savior bids you come,
There is nothing you have to pay,
Be wise and step inside and do not be like some
Who would throw their only chance away.

Unfortunately some will not come because they falsely believe that there are many ways to God apart from Jesus. The Bible however has this to say on this topic; John: 14:16 KJV in Jesus' own words.

"I am the way and the truth and the life, no one cometh unto the father, but, by me."

As long as God allows us It is our hearts' desire to continue our six am, Saturday Morning (Board meeting with our CEO) Christ, the Eternal Orchestrator of our lives. We remain excited as we live with joyful hope and expectations. We want to draw closer to God every day because, we want to walk and live in the purpose for which God has called us. For this to be realized we must continue walking in the footsteps of the crucified Christ.

The crucifixion was the most brutal form of punishment conceived by the Roman Empire measured out to criminals. Jesus was crucified as a criminal though He was innocent to the core. The cross reminds me of how God speacializes in transforming evil into good. In the case of the cross, the good was the purchase of our salvation, and forgiveness of sins through the sheading of the precious blood of His only begotten Son, Jesus Christ.

My friends, there is truly only one way to God, and it is via the cross through the shed, sinless blood of Jesus. Every other blood is sinful. Any other blood would be tainted with sin, and God cannot look upon sin. Jesus' blood is the only blood that covers sin. It is not contaminated by the seed from Adam.

While there is only one way to God, I believe that there are more than one way to Jesus. In the Bible we see where people came to Jesus in many different ways. Nicodemus came to Him by night. The disciples came because He called them. Some people followed Him because He fed them, some because He healed them. Some as in the case of the woman caught in adultery because He forgave them, and some because of His revelation of who He was as in the case of the woman at the well.

Jesus said to His Disciples, "If anyone wishes to come after me, he must deny himself, take up his cross and follow me." Matthew 16:24, New American Standard Bible. Every time I make the sign of the cross on my body, I am reminded that I carry the cross of Jesus in my body. This is the way of the cross. The cross is a brutal thing; it is pain, shame, and sorrow and sacrifice. When we take it up, the life we live is no longer our own. To do that, we must die to ourselves. When we take up the cross, we lift Jesus up in our daily living. Jesus said "If I be lifted up I will draw all men unto me."

The way of the cross is living a life of sacrifice lifting our lord and Savior Jesus Christ up for all to see.

The way of the cross has afforded me the privilege to live my best life now as I wait to do all of God's will here where I live in His Kingdoms on earth, as it is in heaven. Knowing that my name and all His people's names are recorded in the "Lamb's Book of Life.'

Beyond the cross is victory and glorification. One day we will exchange our cross for a **CROWN!**

Like Paul we want to be able to say. "I have fought a good fight, I have finished my course, and I have kept the faith.

Henceforth there is laid up for me a crown of righteousness which the Lord, the righteous judge shall give me at that day; and not to me only, but unto all them also that love His appearance." (2 Timothy 4: 7-8).

I thank God with all my heart that His spirit moved upon my mother's spirit to dedicate me to Him from in the womb.

AMEN!

ABOUT THE AUTHOR

Eisenhower J. Williams (Ike) was born in Jamaica, but now lives in Freeport, Bahamas. It was there after leaving Jamaica in 1987 that he became a born–again Christian, and a member of the Fellowship Union Baptist Church. It was there that he developed a passion to know the Father, Son and Holy Spirit in a sincere way.

Ike is a teacher, a playwright, a stage director and choreographer. He is also one of the founder of Sting Ray Youth Theatre Company, now Performing Arts Alive Ministry. His time is spent in training the youths in the theater in dance and acting and teaching English Language and literature to senior high students.

He is a prolific writer and have so far published three books. "Teaching My Art My Heart", "The Light in Darkness" (a collection of poems) and "Spirit Poems" (another collection of poems), and there six more books and two plays waiting in the wings.

Along with his prayer partner and closest friend, Orson Smith, they have embarked on a journey to diligently seek God and know God in as much as any created man can.

'THE WAY OF THE CROSS' chronicles some of the experiences.

Email:

jike1353@gmail.com

www.ingramcontent.com/pod-product-compliance
Lightning Source LLC
Chambersburg PA
CBHW071215300726
48975CB00004B/1320